The Roux Volume II
J'Parle' Poetry Anthology

Curated by Jerica Wortham

Copyright © 2019 J'Parle' Publishing
All rights reserved.
ISBN-13: 978-0-9990310-5-6

DEDICATION

This book is dedicated to every artist that has ever been hungry for more; and in that desire for more set out their intention, and made every one of their dreams come true.

TABLE OF CONTENTS

ACKNOWLEDGMENTS 7
INTRODUCTION 9
CHAPTER 1 BRITNI SHARDE' 11
CHAPTER 2 LC HARDING 19
CHAPTER 3 RANESHA SMITH 29
CHAPTER 4 DERIUS SKINNER 41
CHAPTER 5 KARMEN S. WILLIAMS 49
CHAPTER 6 TRAI HAWTHORNE 57
CHAPTER 7 A'VAZSHA WALTON 65
CHAPTER 8 CHRISTOPHER ALEXANDER 73
CHAPTER 9 CANDY WEEKS 81
CHAPTER 10 YOUNG MESS 89
CHAPTER 11 RABINA MITRA 99
CHAPTER 12 SOULS INKPEN 107
ABOUT THE AUTHORS 123

ACKNOWLEDGMENTS

I would like to take a moment to thank every author for their contribution to this anthology. I am so proud of each and every one of them for taking a chance on themselves and being vulnerable with you the readers.

To Finally Focus Photography. Thank you for always coming through in the clutch. Your professionalism is epically dope!

Last but not least to my husband Webster, and my children Solomon and Jonah thank you for sharing your time while we worked to make dreams come true. Love you all like air.

INTRODUCTION

Get ready for a journey. The Roux Volume II is collection of thoughts and poetry from individuals from all over the world. Their stories are sweet, sad, and everything in between. While reading I thought about you the reader. Would you be able to digest what is being said?

I think about experiences and stories being shared. Will they be listened to? How often do we negate the words that come out of people's mouths when it requires us to reflect on parts of ourselves?

I thought about expression. Does profanity offend you? If so then turn around. This is not the space for all things conservative. These are the stories of real people, with real emotions, with real ways of expressing themselves. Will you be able to read between the lines?

Why the Roux.. I was called the roux some years ago from my Louisiana friend Beatrice Graham... she said I had a knack for bringing people together. But that it must start from something real good down on the inside. I found resonance in that affirmation. I ran with it. The Roux... this is a collection of poetry and prose. The collection is from unique perspectives of people you may never ordinarily see in a room together. That alone gives me goosebumps, because here they are... together in a gumbo of good reads.

What are the social issues you will find within these pages? What will you do to change them? What parts of human experience will you resonate with? I don't know the answers. I'm also confident these are not the only questions. But I'm opening it up for you. These are artists, remember, they are sensitive about their shit!
Happy Reading,

Jerica

CHAPTER 1
BRITNI SHARDE'

FEET TO SEE..

There was glass inside my carpet and I was annoyed because I couldn't see it...
I thought for sure I'd gotten all of the broken pieces.

It won't matter, if I didn't. or so I thought
Until the tiniest piece effected my feet...

Lamp; sitting next to my bed, I recognized its usefulness.
What a brilliant idea...
I thought to myself.

Days went by... but not a week.
Don't judge me, I can do that.

I am the only human being living in my home.
That's supposed to be a part of the glory of living alone

Finally in my very tiny mildly intelligent mind, I placed the lamp upon the floor.

and then, I saw it there...

The words of the psalmist resonate inside of me and Truth made Himself known.

A lamp to my feet.
A light to my path,

Perhaps, you thought this was about glass...

So this is why He says the Word speaks.
It is alive.
And suddenly, I saw it breathe.

That visual has since, blessed me.

A lamp to my feet;
A light to my path.

ACKNOWLEDGING SIS..

In quietness,
She speaks to me.

Her words cut deep almost to bone and marrow

Occasionally, she's angry with me.
Her frustrations with me are rooted in my responding negligently.
My irresponsibility.

The ability to not properly or adequately respond to obligations pisses her off
She asks that I just do the right thing.

Sometimes she reminds me of my Granny with her sass...
My Mom with her sternness,
all accompanied with Madea's laugh.

She wants me to have a pleasant life...
One filled with joy and laughter
one that honors my people and respects my own person...

To her, God is supreme, mankind is a gift.
Nature is necessary
Water is a natural endowment.

She is held high in space and time...
She has her own way with word and rhyme
She sits with me often... when I read and I find her... she.

She is wisdom.

SOME GUY...

Know thyself, admire thy ways,
Cultivate relationships that don't require trade...
Be more you as you'd let you be...
Careful there... Not to showcase someone else's persona...
An unfathomable depth of space and energy, ideas soul and mind...
He is male, masculine.
Surrounded by theories of a strange amalgam of contradictory traits
made to fit into a corresponding part.
A gentleman.
Undaunted.
Less fear.
But Confidence in the malignant nature of self-flagellation...
Sweet...
Courageous... in stages.
Human unequivocally.
Earth dweller, unapologetically.
Just... some guy.

PRIVATE PARTS.

I reconciled in my soul that I'll be a better human to you...
I won't live in fear of what I've put you through.
My apologies for how I've ignored you...
Only engaging in exchange in an effort to experience pleasure
Rarely seeing you for what you can do...
I've punished you...
Often from a place of emotional immaturity...
I owe it to myself to remember your state of being...
we are separate and equal
One in one and one when tranquil
Private proclaims a place of position...
Submission to a delicacy...
My aim, goal if you will, is to live in a state of mindfulness when it comes to you, body.
You've housed me for years...
You've often worked for me even in those moments that I am diligently, intentionally working against you...
Parts; reveals not whole but pieces, not all but some and as the words flow from the pen, the truth begins to settle in...
I've sinned against you, my own body.
Me, mine, mines... and habitually became one with many...
But He...
In all of His Glory, as He is Holy, was publicly crucified in the same flesh as me...
So that eventually...
after he'd already chosen me...
So intimately...
Citizenry, when they meet me, would experience His Majesty.

SING SOMETHING TO ME...

I thought of a song for you...
Something to draw your mind closer to me and make you smile.
I settled into a mood
"we love so strong and so unselfishly."
said Anita to my soul for you,'
but nerves...
Fear,
Maybe reason...
Led me to reconsider...
Uncertainty...
They crept into my mind and whispered phrases like, "too soon... It is too soon to consider love."
But, it that really fair to my soul?
I settled...
I made the decision that I'll resolve that love is possible.
That sharing such a strength of choice takes courage...
I see your courage...
I see your strength...
And my desire is to honor it,
I told God to help me be kind to you...
That no matter what end we meet at; may He be glorified... Magnified.
I just want Him to be satisfied...
I pray you, dear friend of mine remain steadfast and unmovable despite the tide.
I thought of a song for you...
India said that "it takes time to stay in love's good grace".
So from this place...
I request your mind's eye to rest at the feet of His Majesty.
Trust you are deserving...
Sing something
to me.

CHAPTER 2
LC HARDING

WELCOME TO MELANCHOLY

A fledging he was, seated on the front row of bereavement Baptist before polished sepulcher etched in priestly pretense, incased within its pristine pavilion was the substance of definitive ugly L.C. Sr lain face up face makeup made up dressed to the nines only for six feet it's the dagger of unfathomed unimaginable unexplained morning was the only thing casket sharp from accounts of others I learned of this 1980 morning that I might as well had been the presiding bishop as my perplexed wailing quoted chapter and verse from the book of wake up daddy proceeded by a selection of why God why from the mouth of a babe came perfected peril the weight of my tiny tear drops was all that was needed to propel the avalanche of suppressed droplets baptizing the lashes of every one from the prepubescent pimply faces to the eldest wrinkly water ways perhaps one could have said that I preached my first message that day to this day heartbroken aunts tell the tale of the stirring sermon entitled let it out

Moments later she drove the family car as the sub woofers of my gut wrenching screams bumped to the grave site she hopped out and performed the benediction as we rode away she was the operator of the machinery which covered pappies remains ubiquitous she was though she was the chauffer she was also the unveiler of the fact that I was not seated upon a limo seat but a lap she smiled at me as she hand cuffed my tiny wrist I smiled back with a mysterious look of comfort, and with u-shaped lips and chubby cheeks I muttered GOOD MORNING MELONCHOLY.

BRITANNICA

I stand before my father as he lay in between the ivory white sheets of the I.C.U. I see him unconscious and unaware of the ink of struggle calligraphy written upon his face as it spoke… indicative of pain his awakened lips could not mutter… as I pray over my personal center piece of strength. These glazed over eyes become blood shot at the graphic grief garnered from the grossly god forsaken view. As daddy rests unprivy to all stimuli he is force fed air through a tube and even upon the composition of these words I am unsure if he will pull through. As I behold this painful wonder, I wonder if this unfinished hope book is just a rugged note book, while wondering the possibility of facing the same fate while being viewed by my son to whom my face is 98% identical in my father's face. I see a potentially fast forwarded future taunting an unsure present inflamed form. This optically troubling imagery as the stench of its paint burns into the furthest reaches of my mind. I somewhat align the misfortune of his reality with mine by taking a mental Selah to pause stop and rewind. As I enjoy the rapidly rotting fruits of youth with a partially experienced glare yet a naively focused gaze. I am made aware that these thirty somethings will with a handshake graciously greet the fifties in a hand full of days. As these deceitful years seems slow as the sluggard yet hindsight causes a cheetah swift truth to be abundantly clear. Brevity is breathed upon these days that I have seen for it only feels like 30 minutes ago that I was 15. So to the Lord of ages These questions I humbly ask shall I be removed from this cocoon of self-imposed shame wherein I search for reasons to feel condemned morally filthy and guilty? Or will liberations butterfly wings flutter before I am fifty? Will these leave less branches of perpetual winter become warm comforting and nifty? Will the present storms of today at least give way to flood waters born afresh which dissipate swiftly? Will the faith driven hopes of middle aged predictability uplift me? Or is it unavoidable that these same I.C.U. sheets swaddle me as surgeons rip me and as sickness sifts me? Lord I am not afraid if to see your eyes I should die slow or if my son will see said ink upon my face as the air supply blows just allow me to be an encyclopedia of life well lived before these mortal eyes close before this body is adorned and roses well spread let every volume to my sons be absorbed and well-read after I have breathed my last to enter into the joy of the master may my son quote the words of his daddy's favorite rapper "With that in an egg shell standing at the tabernacle rather the church, pretending to be hurt didn't work so smirk is all on my face like man that man's face was just like my face" so pop after you have lost all vitality and stamina thank you for the lessons down loaded into the tablet of my undeleted consciousness my once living breathing Britannica

"TARRED AND FEATHERED"

I will not be broken, I will not be broken go ahead and let the smoke ascend no matter if flame engulfs me no matter if your petrified beast flees with these tightened fetters tearing me open servant hood is a logic. I could never grasp fear is a language that I have never spoken I will not be extinguished especially by the wicked captures who have done the unthinkable as sport who see me on this black gold and accuse God of wrapping it around something evil and so fiendish. God does not exist in your ships, your forced spirituality, nor in this so called kings English. You so called godly men with such ungodly sin who have drug us here to build your civilization of extravagant lavishness. Men who are inwardly wolves having appetite insatiable and ravenous men who possess such a passion expressed in the filthiest fashion men who possess such gall to label us savages? I hope that you are happy that my body is totally tarred it beats being physically imprisoned and socially barred you have made a foreigner to my own home's tongue, my own home land and to become less than a man but a pawn or an object of totally blatant disregard dipped in darkness a lynching target yet my soul cannot be singed regardless a life full of this injustice is the torture in comparison a momentarily painful death dip your burning tar upon these burning scars let its utter blackness symbolically utter how black you see me. Let these feathers flying light and easy symbolize the wings of angels who perform the good Lord's bidding beyond the realm of human sight welcome me unto the unknown dimension and sacred ascension as we flow into the perfect light honestly I hope that much of what I have learned of heaven eternal was taught in error in terms of what you have forced me to hear for a state of nothingness would be greater than being your servant where among cotton clouds I shall appear as you all partake of these final earthly hollering blood and curdling yells. Please listen for the mumblings of praise as burning flesh you smell as you fools choose to take pieces of my body to use as souvenirs to cherish through the years while I draw near to death at the soundtrack of your circus spectacle cheers. Take my fists as your heirlooms take the remains of my unchained brain which held a made up mind as trash treasure of token just please remember that you had to break this skin to release this king spirit that could never be broken

"THE SMOKE CLOUD"

...... And it shall never come to light until the darkness is exposed, the fact that Willie still lynches and Jim still crows.
In such a festival of falsehood the town of the T has been so peacefully viewed, yet so craftily the red hot spirit of Greenwood's black billowing smoke cloud so subtly presents itself amongst the many energies that this place exclude; the color line, a secret dominion totally covert to the hardened heard of folks fortified in fortune, a painful reality for those suspended in dingy dwellings drowning in destitute desperation, debt, and dead dreams, these are souls with pain thresholds too out of whack to feel the sting or anything but numb to the hurt, you see this place churns out two types. A) Those so soaked in privilege that their minds are blind to the plight of souls clinched tight in the bite of social stigma. Those who see our anger as enigma, the "blackie get over it already crowed", those more sensitive to the preservation of the white whale than that of a black male slowly facing annihilation, or that of a young Latino lady who has had her body violated so much that she doesn't even consider it a violation, or B) people like me who were born on the wrong side of the tracks, unaware that there were even any tracks. Tracks that have been long removed, but even in absence powerful enough to remind the powers that be of what corner of town were destined to be precious and those deemed the home of people not important enough to behold a community improved, the smoke cloud has long disappeared
..... and it shall never come to light, until the darkness is exposed, that in fact Willie still Lynches and Jim still Crows.

KING JAMES AT THE FLEA MARKET

In the darkness of the matter allow me to spark wisdom and hopefully prep the brush to this lyrical art exhibit to the fulgazy types hard is the criticism that I agree with all of marx-isms this one I do kinda sorta.
Bible belts for sale hello? Bible belts for sale half price is this box of pie I the sky if earthly survival fails.
No one is righteous, no not one society of piety we revere what our ears hear preach it pastor! It doesn't matter what is said unintelligible babble will suffice these references of philosophical jargon hardly resonates when your opinion you designate to sheep who want a reality vacay jonesing for a blessed escape. Doctrine doctors don't know enough to educate purple haze praises elevate the high of call and response accelerates no wonder there are so many ex-addicts in attendance ministerial methadone seeking for a feeling and not an understanding of the supernatural architect who subtly constructs of unseen providence into our all too discouraging here and now. Even the unsaved can discern the brainless buzz of the Gos-pill and we wonder why the almighty subject of the lecture is seen as not real. I have been an abuser myself and I know its effects are by far greater than pot, feels good don't it? Real good don't it? Make you want to rain Benjamin's won't it? Destination hell think you can postpone it? When God really shows up He speaks of atonement makes us see our sin and own it. Reveals a truly loving God when we know that we have blown it. His presence is problem solving leading past complacencies nature of revolving teaching us who move forward in him the working together of all things but the pursuit of goose bumps is appalling open garbage bags laid open no draw strings something similar to something over the counter at Walgreen's. All this performing won't produce protection when the darkest clouds are forming not eve a warning from the storming religion, the opiate for the masses bringing no solutions, ineffectual, good to only leave you as is I applaud the temple which still adores his Spirit in it and not the mere venues of get rich quick seminars which feed clergy and leave behind a worthy village longing to ease pains of transient provisions yet having no ability to change their meager condition. Bible bling for sale here chase it with a bracelet or come for a filter for the fallible because indeed everything we hear is not sacred!

CHAPTER 3
RANESHA SMITH

A MOTHERS ROLE

It wasn't the lesson of me teaching my son of how to be a man
It was the lesson me teaching my son growing to a man of how to treat a woman.

Lesson of these are learned at home, define by a mother of what a real woman is and all the good she could bring.
So, when my boys grow they'll know potential
I wanted my boys to view the world different, not to judge book by its cover, and true beauty comes from within.
All shape, sizes, and aspect for them to have not an artificial nor a superficial view
Choosing a woman that loves herself & know that when y'all step.
Y'all step together complimenting each other
Being educated not only in school books but in streets too.
Having a woman of independence isn't a bad thing knowing she can hold her own
Always be a man to practice what you preach, stand for something my son or you will fall for anything.
Teaching my son not just to bring love, trust, and respect to the table but God too; for He is the creator of all things good.
Plus being educated to the fact that respect is a two-way street. No one can really love you nor trust you without respecting you too.
Having a woman on your arm that is believable not pretendable.
Having sobriety, reliability and accountability

As I stated It was never the lesson of me teaching my son of how to be a man

But a gentleman cuz the first women they grow to love is their mothers

SO THEY SAY

I am just another sad black song singing of black injustice.

As if being black in 2018 is somehow better than being black in the 60s. So, they say

Cuz in 2018 no longer do black men die from senseless crime as holding cell phones in backyards.
No longer do black people suffer the injustice of not being able to exercise their 15th amendment rights to vote. Unless you are young black Texas A&M student, or maybe a low-income resident in Georgia being denied the rights to vote early because you were driven there.
Our black sons and daughters are so much free in 2018 from false crimes as Emmett Till. Unless your daughter is selling bottled water on her door steps, or your son is cutting grass, or throwing newspaper. Or maybe…. just maybe your 9year old son backpack brushed up against her and we are shown how free we are.
How dare you use your platform to speak on racial issue, instead of sweeping it under the bed like a 9-year child pretending his room is clean.
"Shut up and dribble the ball" they say
(races white man voice) pick that cotton boy" is what they meant to say

"protest on your own time"
(races white man voice) shut-up and stay in line nigger" is what they meant to say

They have been asking for your papers long before term of illegal immigrant
Everyone loves to dress up and play black until it's time to be black.
Since 1920 black people have been marching, fighting, dying for our freedom and 2018 black people are still dying, fighting, and marching

for our freedom as they try to discredit us as if we were the Cosby.
(foreigner voice)
My people we work hard to get to America for a better life, for a dream, we see your shows, your pop culture, and you black people are lazy and whining.
But it was my ancestors that hung from trees as lifeless dogs, so you can have that American dream; while black people are still dreaming to free cause in the jail system it is just us.
Black people are still under paid, under value, lady Liberty has never shown up for us, she has always been a dollar short, and a day late And America is still breathing that old Charles Lynch: destroy the black mind but keep the body strong; destroying black minds, uprooting schools and community centers in predominate black communities and overflowing them with liquor house, drug, and boarded up buildings trying to destroy hope.
Because only in America:
Can you be black and die from wearing a hoodie and having a bag of candy. And your killer makes money off of selling signed bags of candy and they say nothing.
Only in America can you be black and die for having the rights to carry and the NRA says nothing
Only in America can you be a black female in a stand your ground states shooting warning shots against your abuser, you get the maximum time, and still they say nothing
Only in America: can you be black and die from doing your job and securing a club and still they say nothing.
Only in a America can you be black and go off to serve this great nation and die from helping innocent lives in amall shooting and they discredit you before they honor you.
So they say: I'm just another sad black song but seems to be they just left me on repeat.

STAY WOKE

I dreamt I stayed woke and never walked in a oblivious state again portraying times lines never crossed or yesterday news stayed yesterday

Time can & will repeat living in 2018 yet stories of 1950, 60s, 70s seems to replay my tv screen
News capture horrific slay of Medgar Evers, Emmett Till reincarnated to Eric Gardner, Tamir Rice, Sandra Bland, Terence Crutcher taken unlawfully sparks movements to create civil rights to bonded by black lives matter. Two different eras but we are one in the same.

Resonating hymns echoing in the streets "we shall overcome" giving birth to the millennium black lives matter

Stay woke the movement has never changed only date to seasons

From kneeling at the 50-yard line to the 68' Olympics,
I envision I stayed woke
knowing there's no difference from Fred Hampton to Colin Kaepernick both inspired black minds. See they heard the message and was sold on the dream equal rights, justice, and liberty for all.

We speak different yet we still in the present trying to weed out racism, bigotry, and inequality.
Fearless women as Angela Davis her marches, picket signs and civil disobedience help break the Jim crow transforming our voices to Erica Gardner showing black lives have purpose.

Different day same story still riding for our freedom as George Raymond to the congress steps of Maxine Walters plateauing our fight in the judicial system.

Only time lines change our story remain the same
News flash black America we are the preposition of the word "re"
We redefine the odds, re-envision, recreated trends as Negro history week to black history month.

This upward hill battle may be seen as a pyrrhic victory but never stop moving and growing, we were birth within a culture to break barriers. Our revolution will be televised.... THEY WILL TELEVISE OUR REVOLUTION
Young black minds stay fighting, stay growing, stay motivated to change but most of all
Stay Woke

MY FIGHT FOR YOU!

When did I stop listening to you and tune into me?

Began to feed my flesh losing sight of my race for you

Not the race of morality but immorality on a race I had ran so well
Hearing of the words well done, well done my good and faithful
When did it become just me, and you became obsolete?
When my flesh crept in like a thief in the night and I began to answer its beckon call.
Not realizing it was turning you down on my FM, my Father Message and tuned to automatically me on my AM

Strategizing my own plan, so no longer am I looking for you due to the man in the mirror saying "it was my time, it was my plan, and I'll never wait for hand"
When circumstance became eye level and all I can see was it and not you.
Bills past due, no food, funds, people consistently asking, so I turned it from you. Believing I was winning this rat race on this wheel of life and my assumptions.
Or when did I stop reading for you of my fathers' word? Letting my senses be caught up in the sitcom of this world, in there temper painted predictions, their Crayola drawn up ruling and judgements.
Instead of my father's word:
Wisdom
Order
Righteousness &
Divine divinity

So let me stop, pause, rewind and let my faith formulate my walk. Knowing I look upward and not straight. Knowing He is not in service to

me but I am in service to Him.
He has already told me great is my faithfulness.
Ye though I am caught in my storm let me be caught still. For I shall wait on His promises as David did.
Though I may wait, may I wait and be of good courage.

For you Lord I shall wait as faithful as night turn to day, as faithful as night turn to day.
For you Lord I shall wait

ANGRY BLACK WOMEN

To whom it may concern
Please do not label me for I am not your angry black women.
A woman of confidence he say something with ebony skin tone originally kissed by the sun.
A queen Nefertiti is what he wanted to sit beside him on his throne but then I am told I am too strong, showing any sign of vulnerability means I am too needy, and being educated means I am too opinionated.
Contemplating what is more of the offense: that I am not able to speak with conviction and dictation without your deeming that I am angry.
Or was it the fact my brother sold me out to the other nations with a derogatory statement: that all black women are angry.
On an average we both were born in to the same circumstance: low-income or even a single parent household. The odd were stacked up for me as they were you, I was beat with that same Shepard stick, sat down with the lesson of:
You were born black in this world so what that means is that you have to run a little bit harder, you have to fight a little bit harder, never let them see you cry, never let anyone run over you, and you best dam sure stand tall and walk proud in your blackness. And in this life you need to be educated
But for you my sisters, my daughter, my niece..you…we will always start a leg behind the black man that extra layer of thick is what we need to hold him up when he begins to fall. When the outside world begins to flood in and he is feeling oppressed, depressed, and angry with all the injustice. We are there as black queens to empathize and meet him at his just needs.
But yet we are as a reenactment in history
(Ancient roman voice)
The death of Caesar done in a black woman form.

And we are yet branded again.
We bore the brand of a slave ship, we bared the brand of a slave masters, and now bestowed by my own brother all black women are angry.

What traps and hinder you from seeing all my vast accomplishments, why the incapability of you being able to see past my misplaced smile but yet the story deep within my eyes of the muck and mud we both had to trail through just to stand.

Cain couldn't you see that you and I were just one in the same.
I guess not....
So...
Here is a confession from this black female: Yes I can be angry, yes, I be passionate, as well as I can be loving, king, nurturing, and true....yes, true my attitude can show just as well as unguarded slip.

But riddle me this: have I not earned to express myself as other nations do? But I guess not either.
So to whom it may concern do not label me for I am not your angry black women

CHAPTER 4
DERIUS SKINNER

BROKENNESS

The epitome of rock bottom
Place of despair, heartache and pain
A location of solitude, silence and
A destination filled with time and nowhere to allow it to fly.

But in the same space and opportunity
Blooms the confession of one's own heart and soul
A moment to release all of the desires of that beating livelihood
A foundation that doesn't shake when confronted with the truth

This dwelling of brokenness is a perfect storm,
providing insight to the next steps
or elevator to one's ascension
A higher level that requires growth, change,
And most importantly… faith.

Some hide from the spotlight of brokenness,
But me… I'm learning to thrive…and glow
Separating myself from the shadows and accepting…brokenness

SINK OR SWIM

My arms are bloodied and stiff
From the constant fighting and struggle
Trying to hold on to the ropes that need to be cut.

I've been grasping for air for years…
Seeking the resuscitation of others
Who are just as deep in the water as I am

Yes! I can swim, there's no doubt about it
But when you're in the middle of the Atlantic,
One can only float for so long.

So when I let go of everything,
I sink to the bottom of the sea.

On the way down, as I lose every inch of breath,
I notice the beauty
That lies beneath the surface.

My eyes can't contain themselves
As I see images of the beauty that is rarely discovered
By a shallow man's point of view

I think to myself,
If only I would have chosen to sink instead of swim
I'd have experienced this magnificent life that lies
On the bed…of the ocean floor. Oh what a sight – love.

THE THIRST IS REAL

How is it that
the body is made of mostly water,
But a person can still be deathly thirsty?

Seeking attention that will one day
Quench the loneliness that resides inside

Dehydrated…from the things taken inside
But failing to realize what lies deep
Is all that needed for survival.

Dried up thoughts of who…why, when….and where
Instead of getting nourishment from the Source of Living Water.

You heard the metaphor,
"You can't pour from an empty cup"
Well what if that cup has a hole in it?

How can one preserve what is leaking out,
Slowly falling to the floor

Visible to the eye, no longer held in my hand,
No longer in the cup, but on the floor,
for all to see, and now a hazard to all those near

So why is it that a person can be so thirsty,
When all that is needed is not visible or tangible, but deep inside.

ALONE VS LONELY

Alone – described as having no one else present
Tell me, is this ever really true?
I know that I am never alone because God is always with me – He's omnipresent
But how is it that I am never alone, but still feel lonely?

Lonely – described as sad because one has no friends, companion, or cut off from others
Funny thing is, I tend to do the cutting off
For my own peace of mind, yet I'm still left with
the negative emotions that come with that action.

At what point does loneliness fade away,
And the joy of extroversion climb over the self-built fence of solitude?
For some, they'd rather be alone, but for me….
I'm second guessing if this is truly a choice or a punishment.

Does my past mistakes make me the perfect specimen
For a life of confinement within the four walls of my mind?
Am I damned to a world-class lodging of desolation that checks in every guest,
Monitoring their whereabouts, agenda and at times, forcing their departure date?

Is it me or is it my own security? Alone versus Lonely

UNCONDITIONAL (NSA)

(NSA) No Strings Attached,
That's what I want.
Not a sexual relationship
And definitely not an ad for a desirable companion.

I'm no Pinocchio darling,
and I don't want to be your Giupetto.
Because there are no puppets or woodwork here
Except for these works of art between
My ears and my legs that grow from your stimulus

Why is it so hard to get someone
Who sees me for what I am, can and will be?
Rather than how good in bed I am
Or how much my bank account receipts read.

When can I let down the guard of my soul
So that my equally yoked partner can jump the fence of my heart?
I'm tired of playing guard, jester, and king
When I can just be the emperor
Without worry of attack from an enemy in my own palace

I'm looking for something strange with a lot of change
and that out of the ordinary, spaceships and patty melts type of love.
"That can't eat, can't sleep, reach for the stars,
over the fence, world series kind of love. "

You can't hold back love and it can't be tied down.
It doesn't have a leash and even in a catapult
It springs forward without boundary or restriction
That's what I'm talking about
Unrelenting, unyielding, unshakeable, unwavering, and unconditional
love.

CHAPTER 5
KARMEN S. WILLIAMS

QUEENS, PART I

We are the queens with gravity defying crowns growing naturally from our heads,
We birth the world through our wombs and through chocolate-shaded legs

We are the queens that hold the world on our ample shoulders and nurture the earth with supple breast
We are the queens that stand tall in adversity and bring through all the rest

We are the queens that lift our kings up and rule with a subtle reign
We are the queens with heart to accompany our extraordinary brain

We are the queens that lift other queens with pride and grace
We are the queens that hold our head high and manage difficulty with a straight face

We are the queens

- Karmen S. Williams

PIECES OF ME

A piece of me
Is always with you
Travels on lips and hips
To a sultry rhythm
Fluid and seeping through
Your pores like oceans
Of similes and metaphors
Reverberating like
Sound waves on your
Brain matter
Neurons scatter my
Pieces through pathways
Of your mind
Expanding thoughts and
Defying time
More metaphysical than
Any physical form
Could ever be
Pieces of me take
You on journeys
Both near and far
Move you farther than
Any plane or car
Ever could
A piece of me could
Never be misunderstood
For just a piece
I give you everything
Both the Godly and

The trap Queen
The sinner and
The saint
One sided pieces
I simply can't ever be
All I can offer are these
Words
Strings of adjectives
These nouns and verbs
Let them slide in between
The cover of your ears
Keep you warm
Push back your fears
Fulfill your deepest
Fantasies
My gift to you
These pieces of me

- Tosha Craft

I LOVE YOU TOO

I remember before he hung up, he said, "I love you" and before I could even consider differently, I said, "I love you too".

It's been 123 days, 9 hours, and 35 minutes since I last saw him, not that I'm counting. This is not unusual. It is the nature our relationship. We were never "on" or "off" just no strict lines or titles. We would go for a while without seeing or speaking to each other, but as soon as we did...it would pick up where we left off.

We loved each other, although it could appear different from the outside eye. I just think we aren't ready yet. One day we will be though, one day.

Leonard Deondre Hamilton, we called him "Dre", a 6 foot 3, desert-sun kissed brown skin, thick man, and perfect locks to the middle of his back, knocks on my door at 6:05am with the authority that he was confident was his. I open the door as I can't help but to stare in awe of what the Lord done made. He gives me a smile of straight, white teeth as I melt before him. He laughs openly to himself as he knows the effect he is having on me. His strong, powerful arms pull me into him for an embrace as the essence of him fills my nostrils. I am having a sensory overload at this point. I peel myself from him as he laughs again.

"What are you doing in the bed?" Dre says. "Its 6 am," I say, "I just got in at 4 am." He shows no mercy as he jumps on the bed in which I am laying. He almost immediately removes his shirt complaining of the heat. I have to play as if I did not do that on purpose. I can't understand why he is so hyperactive at the crack of dawn. I am definitely a night owl and he definitely a morning person, how will this work? He decides to go make morning drinks. He says he made them for me because he knows I like the fruity stuff. I laugh and thank him sarcastically. I'm thinking who drinks at 6 am, but a drink with him, by him...I do or at least try. He ends up drinking mine too. He lays his head on my lap and I drag my fingers through his locks and across the smooth skin on his back. He is mildly ticklish and this amuses me so I continue. After a few moments of this, he jumps up almost startling me and sits at the edge of the bed staring into my eyes. He begins telling me of his family and his troubles. We talk it through for a while, before he jumps on top of me still staring in my eyes. If I could only be in that moment forever, I would. He kissed me on my face and on my shoulder so gently, as if to remind me who he was in my life. How could I ever forget?

- Karmen S. Williams

CHAPTER 6
TRAI HAWTHORNE

THE WOMAN IN MY HEAD

The woman in my head tells me she loves me deeply
She won't let me look away when she tells me she loves me
While looking into my eyes.
I'm scared - you see, that she will
See the thing that lives in me.
Torment and torture are their names
They tell me things nobody can hear but me, they show me things nobody wants
To be, they know every single little thing about me
But she – she tells me she loves no matter what they say.
She doesn't say "don't listen to them" or "it's not true".
She just tells me "she loves me".

HEALING

"Going through a healing ain't easy.
So many suppressed and unwanted emotions, towering over a heavy heart, my breathing trying to keep up.
Fearing the stains on my heart will take me over.
I'm going insane and off my game.
It's mental warfare wanting to identify the troubles that still taunt my stained heart.
Can't meditate it away.
I want to give up to my low nature, I know I'll find the answer.
Healing ain't easy I want it to hurry and pass.
So many thoughts wondering what it could be; refusing to take any substance to just face it head on.
If my individuality is gonna break I accept the power struggle over my fate.... Healing ain't easy"

THE WHYS

The whys, and why's for the wise.
Despite my unfaithful plea of thoughts that scar me and were fair to me, you know you don't gotta rely on me.
Or reply to me.
You don't gotta face me, you could even erase me.
You could wish to make a blank of me, but one thing you can't do is; make me hate, despise, or resent you,
Though I you had an obvious clue – I already do.

You were a friend,
You were an enemy,
But even through the periods of hardships and hard tips you were there for me.
I couldn't look at you out of whatever reason,
I felt disgusted for some feelings and decisions.
I lowered myself with false assumptions.
I can peel back the sheets, observe the hints, and you may not be one who sticks around to savor the taste of this situation.

When the stone of life drops, or skips in the soul of man, and causes a distorted ripple in thy perception, the waters come back in tack, and I can see myself clearly again as I once was - *laughing at myself* -my own personal friend.

URGES

I felt the urges, I felt the passions, and I knew that even my feelings couldn't experience the full effect.
I felt the energy, I felt the mental sex, I felt the alchemy, and I experienced so many reactions.
The mood was of the four seasons, and I felt all but couldn't comprehend the reasons.
My sensations were calm and relaxed like falling leaves, my observations from a cold stare felt like the time stopping due to the winter air.
The intensity warmed me up I felt your kiss a rising spring; the fire was lit the heat was unbearable it was indeed the summer though it wasn't terrible.

THE MASTER

Wanting to be seen and heard.
Every word every action.
Wanting to be a political figure to make a difference,
then slowly evolved into wanting to be popular.
Wanting the praise.
Making the decision of wanting to be an attention whore;
just to live up to the expectations of some shit I seen on TV;
some vision.
The vision of division was a goal for my ascension
Unrealistic, though even if I pulled it off it wouldn't be that specific.

Wanting to be distant, and hidden.
Forbidden from the view, and have no clue of who is this "you"?
Wandering alone, I'm grown and that is what is shown from the
bottom to the top of the kings thrown.
An underdog loyal to the low expectations of experienced
pleasures, still off the map like many treasures.
On sale for a cheap price, a bargain yes. However still an over
qualified invest.

"Standing out, without being noticed", an introduction to the
conclusion, an execution of illusion brought by confusion:
good bad right wrong, I realized what kind of drug I was on.
That shit was addictive and explicit.
I wipe away the tears and fears that brought about weary years.
I now swim in the file of sovereignty.
"Standing out, without being noticed", true to me, high as can be.
And hidden low; seen as the master, with a subtle glow.

CHAPTER 7
A'VAZSHA WALTON

DEAR DADDY

Dear Daddy
It's been a long time since I last you.
You know it's been a long time since I last spoke you with.
You see it's been so much I been needing to tell you.
That 14 year old girl is growing up
You see that 14 year old girl been feeling the emotion called rejection,
Rejection!
That seed then planted itself within myself
Rejection you see it grew like weeds.
Dear Daddy
I been kind of lost without you
Rejection just keep reaching me trying to pull me in sucking my mind like a world wind,
I just want to get lost in the wind,
Then replant myself
So I can then redefine myself.
Remember Daddy calling me your sunflower?
Dear Daddy
No lie I take care of business, I even cover my body with modesty,
like your dynasty I'm like royalty
You see I'm a sunflower with a crown waiting to be picked by the right somebody.
(Singing)♫ I just wanna be loved by somebody.....
Yeah right! Not just by anybody
I got picked before by the wrong somebody
You see daddy I cried at night because this somebody left me broke
Literally, jaw broke, heart broke.
I looked up his back in my vision
You see? Rejection keeps fooling me.
Dear Daddy
You didn't reject me

You planted me, watered me, and loved me.
Remember Daddy?
That's before your heart stopped beating
R.I.P you're the real MVP just please remember to save a section!
But first I have to understand this direction God has me in for true understanding
Rejection is only God's protection,
So let me stop questioning what's truly meant for me
I have to stop looking for daddy's affection with wrong directions
Landing in the empty arms of a man that lacks protection for me.

BABY GIRL

A baby girl was born August to be exact, she isn't a star or actress with a film, just memories playing like a movie in her head
Let me take you to the beginning with her being molested instead,
So vivid that memory keep playing over and over again,
Innocent is what baby girl should have been
But instead a grown woman in her head.
She's positioned so that's when fantasies started playing in her head
Baby girl imagine walking down a Red carpet with flashing lights, people screaming I Am A Fan!
But instead she just staring up at the ceiling fan.
Baby girl just wanted to be freed but instead that little girl is lost in a whole different dimension,
So that feeling to get up from that position could die and never be her proposition,
The tension she felt was never her decision, division, missing pieces
You see baby girl didn't have a great start
The story is, family can be an illusion,
That perfect picture on the night stand is just the cover up to a nightmare.

HIGH PLACES

Sitting in high places hiding with loud voices projecting through our TV and hand held devices
With lies filled with greed, always hungry for destruction,
Corruption is their happy meal,
That's the deal,
Dancing with the devil

Sitting in high places snatching souls from underneath us
Not knowing the master plan we go right along with it as if we not against it, is such a clever plan
What's sin to a human?
When an apple is hanging from a tree.
Starving for the truth but end up being deceived
Sorting in high places giving instructions to the deceived because of greed people around the world go hungry when billions of dollars in the pockets of Satan's seeds
Who wants to believe people praising evil powers we can't see, giving instructions on how to destruct things
They called it a conspiracy but I can clearly see the government is being deceived by the powers we can't see
Sitting in high places giving us a false sense of security, strategic, carefully designed to make us lose our mind and question the True Divine
Yin and Yang or Good and evil?
The battle between the two is brutal, portals in and out immortal beings that always keep an eye on us
Although the True Divine is near the devil is right here

THE FEAR

I got to shake this off why does it feel like I'm going to get ripped off 27 with the fear of death
I hate this feeling with a passion, I use black on black fashion to cover up the gashes, despair grips me while I wipe away the tears filled with fear
You see my daddy was only 35 when he met the face of death, took me many years to face the fact I can no longer get the hugs from a strong man I use to think was superman...
But now I see his life was in high demand
I have to shake this off you see this fear get the best of me, the not knowing when it's time to leave
I cringe thinking I could leave my two daughters, too early like my mother left me
You see she used alcohol just to forget it all,
She keeps me thinking what could creep in,
And try to take you just to break you and leave you slowly dying
Just thinking on it got me crying but I know I have to shake this off
Dying young is not an option so I get on my knees and pray for other options
Fuck a notion or the idea that death is near!

CHAPTER 8
CHRISTOPHER ALEXANDER

BLACKS TO THE BACK

Blacks to the back of the bus,
Coloreds eat out back,
No amount of money in this world can turn 'white pie' to nigga pie.
In my pure eyes you are inadequate,
Savages, monkeys,
Thugs, junkies
Ingrates.
A slave with the ability to talk back.
A drivin' miss daisy,
Uncle Tom Boy with a capital B,
Because boy means nigger
in the nicest way.
The following tools will create
Generations of broken spirits far past
Our lifetimes.
Disassociate you with your forefather,
Dispels your need to understand the riches in your blood.
African, Kemites, American aborigines.
If a community knows it's history,
They know the power once held.
Disrupt the home by making its foundation crumble
Make the family's father submissive,
Rape him in front of his woman and children.
Make the woman he loves independent,
Make him watch her be abused,
As he will blame himself at a primitive,
Give her all the power to mold the kids,
Make this man a child hiding behind
coattail of his wife.
Make his body strong,
But his spirit a shell
Easily broken-- hard to repair.
Give them a savior to believe in that isn't theirs,
Instill servitude in the freshly emptied mind,
Promise them an unattainable feat.
Freedom.
Unevenly distribute all power to a specific faction within the community-

Create a fissure amongst this body
Light skin in the house,
Dark skin in the field.
Destroy the ability to trust or communicate,
Systematically teach self-hate.
Repeat.
This combination will make men sheep,
Women lead,
And children emulate.
After a while they'll enslave themselves.
Lay out this plan
Commit and
The return pay will be well.

WISDOM

Hear the repeating songs from the catacombs?
Wisdom-
The equivalent is
Knowledge times failure plus the action of living,
Divided by the time given before this breathing star becomes a mirage
in vision;
Intangible-
Lost in translation of our generational compass.
Pride has a decay rate
Of a hundred
When being meek isn't confused with being humble.
Me to me:
Stumbling is not falling
Nor halting.
Stopping is only tangible if laying still
Is still an option;
Little rain ain't never hurt nobody,
Dance to the rhythm of thunder-
Pose like you're lightning
Stretching across the sky-
On the blackest of nights;
Contrast enough to spark in the dark.
Started as a flicker
This little light of mine,
Be Blinding;
Shine like burning tinder will
Never become ash and embers-
Remember:
Being a beacon of light allows space for emulation.
Imitation is the fondest form of flattery-
Happily taken
For shining bright is an explanation of
Enlightenment.

FLY ON THE WALL

Let me be a fly on the wall of your vulnerability;
An agent for still waters to make wake and waves,
Quivering and shuttering like spring leaves
After a crisp rain-
Let me be the pleasure of each season for your elation-
I'm a love sick patient;
Needing to be doctored
With your touch healing ailment.
Allow your flower to blossom under the galaxies backdrop;
Stars twinkle to our cycle of excitement.
Peaking at mountain tops and swooning with valley lows.
Lean into me;
Allowing the pleasure between us to ache like growing pains
Creating a strain on our ability to be rational.
I never believed in momentary eternity
Until you showed me the depth of your ocean.
Let me plunge to a depth undiscovered
Recovering pieces of you uncharted,
Unguarded.
Restarted;
Rekindle the spark that initially started the blaze-
I want to suck the nectar from your lips
Like the sun kissing moisture from grapes.
Nibble your thighs as they tremble;
Plain and simple
I want to dismantle your temple
Temporarily.
Addicted to the validation of your groans as I reconstitute your altar
Sacrificing flesh, heaving breath, and sweat for your appeasement.
Paying tolls one stroke at a time
Can't rush that!
Let me be your rejoice;
The spine tingling out of body pilgrimage
To the center of the you-ni-verse.

MANIACAL

Maniacal(adjective)
exhibiting extremely wild or violent behavior.
My mood swings accelerate as the hours become later,
Fidgety-
I got a best friend in my head waiting to get out;
Spout out a shout out
from the beast locked within.
Wits end is a dingy place-
It had me standing at the void in the mirror with a gun to my face
Hysterical cackling shuddering babbling
do you really think it's a game?!
I wear a red nose to distract from my pain
Now it's simply a joke.
Insert a Robin Williams quote.
"All it takes is a beautiful fake smile to hide an injured soul."
A gentle smirk hides my short circuited mental constitution;
Up with the moon's twilight,
Lacking cognition or ability to take action
Idly clutching fear as understanding evades me.
I crash like head on collisions;
Veering to isolation
Fix me
I need to be regulated.
Pharmaceutical soup
My doctor is the dope man
Look at the flick of that pen stroke-
Peddling pills to po folks for the love of money.
I pay insurance
To maintain the experimentation.
Black, poor, and mental so I'm expendable;
Pass me over,
I'm no more than a statistic to you.

FREEDOM

Freedom(noun)- the state of not being imprisoned or enslaved.
The liberty bell cracked because freedom was not sustained;
It did not ring liberation,
Unalienable rights were not upheld in it's name.
Sovereignty held over the land belonging to mother earth--
It's native dwellers devoured by disease.
Extinction of landrace beasts-
Bison, bird, fish.
Frack till the earth is coloured piss,
Wells from groundwater can no longer exist.
Resist?
Futile in practice,
Industry is eating the planet,
Leaving waste in wake.
Freedom does not equate pillage,
Does not define ownership,
Does not create order.
Freedom is peace in chaos-
Time, matter, and space
Allowed to crash and flow at no pace
Created by hands.
Freedom rings the loudest from bloody brows.
Worn muscles.
Rubble.

CHAPTER 9
CANDY WEEKS

HIS LOVE

His love spread thin
Across every lie ever told
Across everything he was doing
But blamed me for...
His love spread thin
Still in love with another woman
Maybe ten...
His love spread thin
I spread my legs when
I should have guarded my heart

Cj2010/1

ITS MINE

It's my peace he wants
When a relative almost passes
It's my peace he wants
When everyone around me seems fake
It's my peace he wants
when my child and I have disagreements
But who knows that's normal
It's my peace he wants when x's call
Regretting past mistakes
It's my peace he wants when at work
My manager is a jerk...
It's my peace he wants
but cannot take
that's why he keeps trying to throw obstacles
in my way
he's defeated Monday through Sunday
by the blood of the lamb
he cannot defeat me
because I was predestined, pre-ordained
I am apart of God's plan
The enemy fails to understand

THE STORY OF: CLOSE BUT NO CIGAR

The guy I dated was not the man I first met
So, he apologized for his wrongs
But justified his actions
Respected my values
All except for my celibacy
Spoke of love, faithfulness and
Staying
However;
Walked out
several times
and...
took me shopping for wedding rings
he couldn't afford.

TORN.MENT

Fear of rejection for
The good in you
Shining through versus the bad
Girl he wants you to
Be, careless, carefree…
Party girl not wifey or
Wife to be.
Then they hit ya with
That "I see why you're
Single" and "you can't
Turn a hoe into a house
Wife", anyway girl go
Put on that skirt girl
I love it
When you show that
Skin. While he looks
At that chick walking
By who may be a
Bit more thick or a
Little bit more thin
Causing your self
Esteem to wear
Again, no, not again
I love him?

7/5/11

HIGHER GROUND

When younger I didn't feel roots
I was oblivious to what was going on
around me.
My soul wasn't anchored,
I was loved but everything was moving
So fast I was drowning.
Literally
I had a nice job, place, car but I lived in the bar
in my 20's.
Now that I'm older I wanna
Make a home with the souls I let in
My life.
That's why you can't sit and
Eat with everyone you meet. Everyone
Was born into darkness but it's the ones
Who carry the light that you seek.
The mission is to then plant the light to be
God's hands and feet.
To deny those dying
Would be like he never carried me.

CHAPTER 10
YOUNG MESS

WEAK IN THE KNEES

Class in session pay close attention you f******with a veteran
Kamasutra is the text and the subject is sexing
I'm might even be nice enough to even let you make a suggestion on the lesson
Feel my... Breathe on YO neck I put my... tongue on your flesh
Slightly ...nibble on YO neck I got you... wondering what's next
As I kiss on YO chest
Now my ego upset but I don't leave them upset...
you can check my stats I'm bout 90% success can't please them all
Use my teeth to undo your bra
grip your ass slip off your drawers
Ten-Hut now I'm standing tall put your hand on it as I wonder do she run or can she take it all
kiss on your left bosom lick the right
Then I suck on your nipples wishing I had some ice.
Lay back relax it's going to be a long night
Work my way past your abdomen down to your navel the tips of my fingers slowly slidin down to yo peach
I peak
its neat
I sniff smell clean
Bring that drip for my fingertips to your lips like tell me if this taste sweet
then I do what I do and you do too
you know you taste me and I taste you

skip to the next scene and now I've entered you slow stroking intervals
stirring the pot like stew and all you keep hearing you say is oooooo
you moaning I'm groaning you secreting more juice
And I'm just jumping into puddle like a kid with galosh boots
The momentum is rising u tryna throw it back but meeting you at every stroke tryna break your back

You say faster
You say harder
But I'm in control of the motion lemme.... switch up the tempo and go back to slow stroking
See I don't want the hillside I want the Mount Everest peak
Can I dive in your ocean like Jacqeez short stroke half stroke then I dive deep the call Mess they don't call me neat
Now that I've done as I please let's do what you asked
turn over legs up put this pillow between ya lower back and ya ass(thought I was too young to know 'bout that)ok now let's see if I can find that spot that takes us to ecstasy,
Stroke around a bit until i fill it gripping on me,
Then I dip in that thing, It's getting wetter but I keep dipping...till I slip in that thing, my leg cramping…
Bitch u bet not give out on me.
You slide back into the headboard now I'm climbing that tree, u say don't stop
And I can feel u start trembling.
Your legs shaking feel like the earth quaking
I got a few more Strokes left in me
And I came to please I feel this sensation tickling me
'Bout the same time yo lips tighten to a squeeze
And I just can't hold this thing so fuck it we peak on 3
1 2 3 and in sync
We release weak in the knees

BEHIND CLOSED DOORS

She a queen and I'm a king
But that don't mean it's meant to be
When it's just you and me seem like nothing comes between
But when we not....
It's a completely different thing
Like we living in a dream
You shouldn't have to compete
So I leave
I'm knowing that ya heart is on ya sleeve
I tell ha don't jump cuz it's way too steep
She on the brink she like "fuck it I'm a leap"
I'm a dog: but she swearin I'm a sheep
In disbelief and the truth cut deep
Even thou she number two
I'm still calling her at 3
Cuz it's where I wanna be
That's my lil baby and she listen when I speak
And I don't gotta say a thing she know exactly what I mean
She on my mind so I'm trying not to think
I'm in too deep
I'm 'bout to sink
When I'm with her I'm at peace
And that's the only time I sleep

I'M THAT NIGGA PART1

My name is Mess and I'm that n****
Been that n****
Gone be that n****
My service in high demand it might...
Take me a minute to get with ya
Tell you why
Because I'm that n****A
G and a gent is a beautiful mixture
Don't think my ego can get no bigger
Probably why I feel like I'm that n****
Naw better yet...
I know cuz no matter where I go feel as though I'm the bigger figure
Maybe just maybe I am that n*****
Yeah yeah that's right I feel it now
I'm nice on the mic all I needed was a double shot of Remy
No ice
Straight to the head
Yeah that might make you quiver
But I take it like a champ
cuz I'm that n****
I'm cold as retro
Might give you the shivers
Yeah I know last time I hit the stage I gets the jitters but somebody
fucked up and told me I was that n****
Since then I done got a little richer
But not that much dont jock a nigga
fill my head I might think I'm poppin
Nigga riding my wave they can't stop a nigga who that was said he was better?
Ha STOP IT NIGGA

THAT NIGGA 2

Somebody told me I was getting cocky
Well if you feel I'm out of line I welcome you to try and stop me
I see nobody moved that's cool I guess
I am that dude let me reiterate how I been that nigga
Gone be that Nigga so you don't get it confused
Thousand pardons if you think me rude
But move bitch
I'm tryna get through
I'm popin they stop me
Lil Mama like skews
Then she apologizes and goes on to tell me how she don't mean to intrude
But I seem pretty cool. And blazay blah and blazay wool
Cut her off to let her know this ain't what you wanna do,
I'm cocky as fuk and I know I'm that dude,
Do you know what I could do to you.
You ain't heard about the last few
Let's skip the interlude
I'm going to tell you the truth
I will fuk yo whole world up boo
I mean you grown do what you want to
But I'm telling you now I ain't shyt
So later, don't play the fool
cuz my only reply is going to be you knew
See I'm THAT nigga
A divine playa from the Himalayas like my playa patna Jeromey Rome
First born son the 4th one rightful heir to the thrown
That make me that nigga in this here town
So all you mere mortals need bow that as down
See I'm still that nigga gone stay that nigga
Might be never if I ever get wit ya
Cause currently I'm posted like a like fixture

Moving the decimal place and increasing my figures
You prolly to small minded to understand the bigger picture
Even if I painted it wit ya therefore.....
I ain't goin back and forth with you niggas
Cuz I am that naw damn that who he say he portray
He or even claim he be
ME
That nigga that is dude tripping my nig
I'm that nigga true but ain't no buffoon
I ain't yo porch monkey nor am I yo coon
Not no uncle tom
Sale out no
And I no negro on the down low
NAW I ain't none of them bro
I'm that nigga
If you ain't know
Well here it go
Check the flow
I'll check ya at the door pull up wit the Lawn mo
And that even my regular JO
I Go Bro
I know I am that nigga
Didn't come to brag didn't come to boast I just came to let all muhfuckas know
I'm real as fuck they know what I'm bout
When I step in the room I'm dripping with clout
Let me say this and I'm out
My lips bigger, my dick bigger,
If I fuk with you I'm stuck with you
You mighta missed it earlier let me say it clearer
I AM ......

G EGOTRIPPIN

I don't compromise If it compromises my integrity
I could give 2 fucks If you think one bit less of me
Used to be short term now focus on longevity
The residual income that brings financial stability
Tryna capitalize off my abilities and feeding off the synergy
Only positive vibes you knowj ust centering my inner chi
See cause it's a daily struggle to check the inner me
Best you stay in yo lane u might unleash my inner g
If it ain't profit or for the culture then it's a waste of my energy
The nerve of these clowns
Could you believe they tried to limit me,
Like I ain't already know that perception is reality,
And plus I wrote it down so im manifesting my destiny
Really with the shit I just verbalize intellectual
Y'all these nay sayers and haters tryna gimme the teal
Tell em I got the juice so I don't need yo drink
What did old boy sa yI'm going to get what's mine eventually,
And I ain't trippin off what ain't meant for me
If it's meant to be then it will be
Used to Tennessee the Hennessy
Got a lil money now its Remy V.... S.O.P.
Work from 6 to 6
And then from 6 to 6 I'm chasing and cheese
Rick Ross ain't got shit on me
Everyday I'm hustling see
My father and his father laid the foundation for me
So it's safe to say at Birth I was already royalty
Not to mention my mom's reign supreme
Respected as the queen
So I can say honestly I'm a product of a Dying Breed
But just cuz you come from greatness that don't mean that's what you going to be

I'm 10 toes down on my own two feet.
Doing what I got to do to make sure that my children eat
They didn't ask to be here so I owe them everything
Nerd status.
You see the glasses ain't no need in you testing me
If you ain't wit me you against me
But i advise you to invest in me
Hell the return is guaranteed
It's not marketing, pyramid, nor Ponzi scheme
This the real thing
And you know like I know ain't nobody fucking wit me I'm a G.O.D. at least by definition #3

CHAPTER 11
RABINA MITRA

GRACE

She was bright and brittle,
just like a star about to die!

She braved, black waves
and her heart like a mourning cloud,
Cracked. Often.
Sounds of silence dragged her down the dark dungeons,
young wounds gushed.
Flushed,
She waded past hard nights,
As moonlight filtered through rains,
She whispered an elegy,
Her pains swirled,
with the sharp, cold blade between her breasts, she waited for him on a
jagged cliff one last time!

A soft kiss on her lips,
And she flew!
splattering hot blood on the face of the dawn,
It was a beautiful mess!

He stood there, as the crimson sky weighed down on him..
Yes, he had once misspelled grace!

THE WOUND

I seek no cure,
It's too late now, anyway.

So I let it drip
Blood squirts,
My tongue licks,
salt.
The wound opens.
Like a budding flower.
Soft at the core.
It's Rose-red shade.
Wet.

My face is black.
This is what I lack-
The Calm.
And the pain digs.
Deep beneath my bones,
It spreads.
The rot.
Germs fester.
The brown seeds multiply.

I hide this wild garden inside,
With all the budding pinks and thorns.
My veins cry blue,
My heart loosens
Like a thread running in wrong directions,
From its grey spool.

It's not easy to carry,
What's been so deeply buried
Under layers of indignations.

The wound seeps.
The wound lives.
The wound loves.

Love, is a wound.

FAIRY-LIGHT

I break my bones into fairy lights.
Sea-snores line up my consciousness...
I feel free to love,
Your fingers trace up empty spaces between words...

Fond colours seep,
deep under hot skin,
pain seethes.

I feel.
I crave you beyond all meanings,
As a child craves to understand,
How daylight turns into something so unfathomable as darkness...

BELOVED

I have now, grown too fond of the grey dawns,
that look me in the eye with no promise
Of sun!
My heart has been, always, a stormy place,
A wet land, ravaged by winds, lashed down by hard rains.
Still love thrived here.
Fierce yet free for you. Boiling at times.
Beloved!

Sometimes my soul leaks,
And what remains is my sad insect body, floating, in a gleaming pool of blood!
I have visions of you burying my inert wings,
Whispering prayers,
Throwing rose-petals in air and cursing the bad wind.
Relief flooding your limbs as you return to an emptiness,
A white, erased void, waiting to burst out colours!
I see you there often, laughing and crying!
Creation suits you. Best.
Beloved!

I wish not to be forgotten, No.
I shall leave traces. The scent of my tears.
The taste of my heart on fire.
The echoes of my silences.
You must find me once in a while,
In the forest of your dreams,
My demon-face. My angel-face.
And put me to rest, in your arms.
Make me sleep in the shade.
Beloved.

I promise to dissolve in the chill of the air.
I promise to thin out, when greater pleasures invade you,
I promise not to come back, crossing the thresholds of death,
When life fills you with blessings to the brim.
Until then, seek me for a heartbeat or two.

"Beloved."

HE IS JUST ANOTHER MAN.

They kept her , like coins pushed to the deepest end of pockets,
like a broken toy, forgotten,
inside an old drawer.
But they kept her still,
Sometimes digging her out from the damp, black depth of fabrics,
or rescuing her from dust and cobwebs.

She only dreamt of his face.

They used her, when their time suited best.
like a penny, spent her to buy cheap beer.
wiped her face, brushed her hair,
dressed her in silk,
coloured her lips.
painted her nails.
Then they mounted her,
and mad vultures crowded inside her head.
They flapped heavy wings, and the air under their feathers smelt of
countless hard deaths to come.

Still, she hoped to hold his hands and fly.

Hairy hands groped at her softness.
She didn't resist anymore.
Her body disowned her and flowered under assault.
She couldn't understand her body.
And everyone
misunderstood well.
So,they kept her.
like small change in pocket, tossing her in the greedy palms of wealthy
beggars
Who had her in turns.

She lied motionless,
and in her eyes floated a road,
sides of it lined by trees.
and at the end of the road that face.
tired but happy,
deep lines of struggle etched in his smile.
She smiles, as they beat her body down.

They kept her.
Like a dying firefly in a jar.
her dull blinking light was still an amusement.
Until that moment, when His face came down on hers.
And kissed her to death.
His smooth hands ripped red silk,
His marble body crushed her womb.
The fire in his eyes burned her skin.
"He is just another man"
shouted every cell in her head,
And in a bed of scorched dreams,
under an elaborate sky,
She slept. Dead.

Regards.
Rabina Mitra.

CHAPTER 12
SOULS INKPEN

KLANSMAN

My fight is hereditary
You see me as a terrorist but I feel I'm the countries blessing.

My ancestors made it possible to be who I am
For we have kept those in check that would one day try to ROB and ROCK this wonderful nation...

Those mongrel races

I still remember the day when that MONKEY GOT ELECTED!!!

ALL I DREAMT ABOUT SINCE THAT DAY IS HOW IT WOULD FEEL TO WRAP THE NOOSE AROUND HIS NECK, HANG HIM FROM A SYCAMOR LEAVING HIM AS STRANGE FRUIT FOR THE SUN TO DRY AND STRETCH AND....

wait...I'm getting all worked up again...I see the world as I know it has been made right

We now have someone that will take care of the whites and now it's time...

"make America great again"

Let's

"Make America Great Again"

Get rid of all of the Mexicans

Split them up from their families but rebel flag waving redness wanna get mad at the system when CPS steps in to take their kids from a meth infested crib

Lets

"Make America Great Again"

Wait wait wait

We can talk politics when it appeals to you but I say
"Black Lives Matter" and all of a sudden I'm being typical
and when I don't agree to always back the blue then I'm being racist...

well look at you standing all white and mighty

Can't I be both part of BOTH factions or did that NEVER occur to you?

I say "Black Lives" you say "All Lives" I scream "BLACK LIVES" YOU THINK "GANG TIES"
I cry "my life" you say it's all right
But how can that be so when I'm guilty at first sight?

We should stop talking about this because I will blow veins listening to your ignorance

Because you can't fathom what it's like to be on the other side of white...oh wait lemme guess you're one of those blue eyed blonde haired Indians...

FUCK outta my face

It's better to be thought a fool than to open the mouth and remove all doubt

VELVET VOICED KING

We here in Muskogee were witness to many a thing

We witnessed the fall of black businesses during the massacre on Black Wall Street

To gentrification of our small corner of this Muskogee nation when a mall was put up where once peoples hallways stood.

Stores bustled and folks hustled where once black men and women cuddled

Cries of babies and children playing now muffled because the system gave no leeway for the families to struggle and/or fight back

Muskogee has seen some things

Muskogee has seen some things like a Velvet Voiced King known as Lansing

See

"Some of you know and some of you don't know"

Echoes through eternity because some of you were privy to how it felt to hear him speak while others paid no attention like you had better things to do

SOME OF US KNOW while others WISHED THEY KNEW!!!

I would geek as soon as his name was spoken and I was able to hear his speak REGARDLESS of HOW many times I heard how

"That was no woman that was a beast"

See I KNEW when I was a wee lad that we had time to sit in the presence of a king even if he sat in his throne room writing grants or in his army cammies

I was present for EVERYTHING

See y'all don't understand Muskogee has seen some things

I wished he could see me one more time get up on stage to do my thing because I would shout out to him

Thank you for leading the path, just know your courts are NOT left in wanting, thank you for setting a fire for us to follow....

Thank you for being that

Velvet Voiced King

THE OPPORTUNITY

I'm obligated to the opportunity I've been given

It's a God given talent and definitely a challenge to be able to place yourself in someone else's shoes
by giving a little piece of...you

That's a life worth living

I'd say the task is easy but it would be spitting in the face of the greats

One could almost say it's effortless what we do as poets, on might wanna say it's almost like breathing

By the same token someone could say it's like competing
Your minds moving at paces only rabbits feet move and your hearts trying to keep up and your soul cries out

"Yo you need to work out dude"

Your fingers feel like fire, wrists locked up like criminals.
Pencils written down to the erasers while pens exploded from the pressure we put them through

So tell me, who THIS is easy to?

So yes I'm a slave to the mind, my heart is the machine and I am an addict obligated to the opportunity

Addicted to telling stories, obligated to tell truths
But what I find most satisfying is when I write something

JUST FOR

YOU

SOULS INKPEN

-NARCOTICS ANONYMOUS-

My name is Brandon Current and I'm an addict.

I wish I had a good report to tell you guys today but the truth is...

I'm sick.

We all know the story or at least what "they" say

"Once and addict always an addict."

I was 16...

16 when I took my first hit and I gotta admit I was hooked no bullshit.

People used to see me searching the stars like I was that guy from the movie...you know the one???

"A beautiful mind"

In time they'd see me crawling through yards and cars in and out of bars looking for a piece just to ease...

my pain

I was going insane and needed a quick release, something I could squeeze to offer some sort of relief in the form of...

peace.

Now I'm 33 and for awhile I was clean, but here I go again on the fringe trying to get what it takes to make me feel more like...

me

I'm trying to find more cause...

I wanna be able to fly free and I stand here at this podium telling you all MY harsh truth, that I'm an addict just like you.

But I'm NOT trying to be freed

you see these meetings were made to help you while they're only hindering me.

I want...NO...NEED THIS!!!

When I'm in department & grocery stores I probe the isles in search of it.

MY SKIN CRAWLS AT THE VERY THOUGHT OF IT, MY MIND GETS TO GOING AND MY HANDS START TO TWITCH, MY SOUL LOSES CONTROL EVERYTIME I GET THAT ITCH!!!

It's something I Can't Describe to have it churning inside causes me to throw fits.

YOU call it drugs and I say yea that's true indeed.
My oratory euphoria my mental methamphetamine
My beautiful syringe of soliloquies...

"THEY" CALL IT DOPE
while I simply call it poetry
"THEY" CALL IT SICKNESS
and I say it's the cure to me.

I'm NOT HERE TO GIVE YOU A SPEECH OF "TOGETHER WE CAN ALL QUIT!!!" I'm here to tell you it's YOUR life, YOUR addiction, YOUR SUFFERING IF YOU CHOOSE TO GIVE IN!!!

Keep listening to what "they" say and see how far you get.

But as I leave this podium, know that I plan to go forth with this, cause as "they" say...

"Once an addict always an addict."

And I absolutely refuse to quit, because I'll NEVER give up what gives me my identity...

I'll never quit doing poetry.

© 2016

~SOULS INKPEN~

DAUGHTER OF A RAPE VICTIM PRODUCT OF A HATE ISSUE

Made to feel ugly inside but on the outside miss lady
Was absolutely beautiful

You would think she was the free spirit her outter shell showed her to be

but truth be told she was dying from internal injuries...heart bleeding profusely due to lack of

Love

She was hated by most including the ones she held close...those SAME ones who were supposed to say

"Baby Come Close and allow me to show you, let yourself loose I'm always here for you"

She became damaged goods.

lost at the beginning from a fucked up birth
She wasn't supposed to survive long enough to see the Earth

Her mother found out too late so the money was no good when she went to see the nurse.

She had initially attempted suicide taking pills to let slip her mind on that final ride cause she couldn't deal with the issues of being...

raped

Next came the idea of a self medicated abortion
Some messed up way using a contorted coat hanger

She felt it was okay because
She would be pregnant again...
One day...the right way

But when it came down to the deed she was too deep into the seed growing from within to let it all end.

THAT PLUS

She fell for what was supposed to be

Love

Until this man told her

"It's not mine and you can't make me, I'll be damned if I take care of rape victims baby"

So she went to the clinic the next day begging the doc to make everything okay but she was too late and this baby was to be raised by nothing more than

Damaged goods

Back to the story and I know this may seem boring

but if you search your friends deeply you may be staring at a diamond that's cut roughly

Just too deep for your eyes to see

This "natural beauty" couldn't take the pain any longer being the

"unloved princess" kept in distress awaiting a knight in shining armor locked away in her four walled Castle known as her

Mind's Eye

She used to get high attempting to ride the tides of life's Untold Lies made into dreams though all she sees are

nightmares

This...

Daughter of a rape victim product of a hate issue

Father wore football pads and drunken laughs, he had just enough to mask the last act that made this Woman's figure broken down to Mere shit

A daughter's visuals of a world made into Bliss all torn down turned into piss

She attempts to end this

This lie she's reminded of with every Blow from her father's fist

She attempts to end this

This lie She re-lives with every touch of lust from her stepfathers lips and EVERY touch of FUCKED UP FROM EVERY THRUST OF HIS HIPS

She attempts to end this

This disease of inner hatred she receives with every look of disgust from her...mother's eye
When all she wanted was to be the twinkle inside

She ended it with one round from a 45
And you wonder why

Daughter of a rape victim product of hate issue...

look at how peaceful she appears in the basket lined in satin
I'm tired of crying someone give me a napkin
I'm tired of the sorrow I'm tired of the struggle

I wish we could have met so you knew somebody loves you

SOULS INKPEN

ABOUT THE AUTHORS

L.C. HARDING

L.C. Harding has been a poet since his early elementary years. He has always found it relatively easy to convey deep thoughts and opinions in a fairly artistic or deep way. During his early years he found joy in writing children's books and short stories, but it was during his pre-teen years that he discovered the power of storytelling, dark emotion, rhythm and whit that his fervent appreciation of hip-hop music sparked within him.
As a proud product of north Tulsa Oklahoma, L.C. gained a quite a reputation from his middle and high school peers as a developed M.C. As of late L.C. has found an even greater thirst for crafting art with a faith based and urban synergy however, he steps outside of those limits to express commentary relating to the state of man kind as a whole. L.C. feels most inspiration in work that reaches out to those who experience the loss and burden of losing it all and having to rebuild their worlds from scratch.

BRITNI SHARDE

Britni Sharde is a writer poet and photographer. Her heart's desire is to showcase the nature of God through the arts and in how she lives and loves. She is an alumnus of Wiley college in Marshall Texas, and Oral Roberts University in Tulsa, Ok, where she currently resides

DERIUS J. SKINNER

Mr. Derius J. Skinner is a multi-faceted entrepreneur and change agent dedicated to social justice reform and community enhancement. A Louisiana native and proud New Orleans Saints fan, Derius started his journey to educational advancement as an alumnus of Wiley College, a Historically Black College in East Texas. During his tenure, Derius joined the elite Alpha Phi Alpha Fraternity, Inc. He later embarked on a journey through corporate America with a career that has spanned nearly 10 years at Bank of America.

Derius expanded his knowledge by earning a Bachelor's Degree in Psychology and Master's Degree in Organizational Leadership from Argosy University. In 2016, Mr. Skinner relocated to Coral Springs, FL and has served as a leader within Bank of America Merchant Services. Derius has exhibited civic responsibility through the formation of the Black Leadership Network in his organization, as well as serving the community as a Youth Director for Church by the Glades of Coral Springs, FL. In addition, Mr. Skinner shows his passion for Jesus Christ through fellowship and the creation of the podcast, "For the Christian Culture." Derius believes in conveying ultimate love of God and genuine concern for others as the main tools for helping one another reach new heights.

Derius cites his inspirational figure as Langston Hughes. During times of adversity, Langston used his passion and gift of words to unite a world so intent on dividing American culture.
"Hold fast to dreams, for if dreams die, life is a broken winged bird that cannot fly." – Langston Hughes

MARVIN SMITH IV AKA YOUNG MESS

Marvin Smith 4th A.k.a (Mess) Is a 29 year old Tulsa native. Grandson to Mr. Marv of Marv's club and son of Messey Marv of Retro Grill & Bar.

Mess hosts a many of skills and talents including; Audio Engineering, Machining, Poetry, Paint & Body, Advertising etc.

His debut to the stage was open mic at, none other than J. Parle. Debuting his feature poem "IM THAT NIGGA" at J. Parle's Ego Tripping he has since featured for Mr. Metaphoria and Velly Vel.

Embarking on his musical journey Mess recently opened Mess N Wit Music Studios, birthed from Mess' Mobile Music. He Is also the Floorman at Retro Grill & Bar and owner of #NOMESSLAWNCARE.

Fueled by drive, determination, and the phobia of boundaries in Music, Mess pushes the limit on the "Norm" and follows no protocol.

KARMEN S. WILLIAMS

Karmen S. Williams is a California native and raised in Oklahoma. She has lived and traveled to various lands experiencing and learning from cultures. Karmen being a true introvert, has been writing thoughts, poetry, plays, and stories since she learned to write. She received her doctorate in 2016 and is currently a public health and health services researcher. Karmen is naturally optimistic and uses this art form to convey hope and vision of great possibilities to the human race.

CHRISTOPHER ALEXANDER

I'm Christopher Alexander; I'm a poet and I've been writing poetry since 2014. I write about tribulations I face that are relatable for myself and my community. Writing gives me a place where i can be vulnerable without judgement.

A'VAZSHA WALTON

Just a sunflower with gold sparkles on top.

RABINA MITRA

Her soul glides and seek the fragrance of monsoon. She makes hymns out of unreturned loves. An Indian girl, who smells awfully of old paperbacks, and is addicted to 'petrichor'! Both the sound and the smell. She is a lousy speaker, so she writes and writes, of the storms, stars and staples. Music envelops her nights and days, she builds castles of words, destroys them to build more. A selenophile, moon melts and flows through her veins. A lover of waters and woods, the first sunrays filtering in through the leaves. Poetry makes her, breaks her, takes her to the world beyond.

RANESHA SMITH

Ranesha Smith is a fellow graduate student of Tulsa Community College and is currently seeking her bachelor's degree at OSU-Tulsa. Ranesha has been showcased at several poetry lounges in Tulsa, Oklahoma. She has appeared at the Oklahoma Jazz Hall of Fame (2010), Saltys (2016) and JParle (2012 & 2018). Her poetry reflects what matters to her most, which is her family, her faith and speaking on African American awareness issues. Ranesha can be contacted on: facebook.com/Ranesha Smith

BRANDON CURRENT

Hello my name is Brandon Current, but for all intents and purposes you can call me SOULS INKPEN.

I hail from a small city in Oklahoma called Muskogee, I'm the youngest of 3 ALL of whom have served or are still serving in the United States Marines and while their are 3 of us, only my mother, my older brother and I write poetry.

I've been writing since I was 16 and failing at love, I've been spitting since I was 23 and serving abroad.
I've longed to belong to something bigger than myself, so forming the Muskogee Soul Searchers was one of those endeavours and NOW...I give parts of myself to you.

TRAI HAWTHORNE

Trai Hawthorne, born and raised in Tulsa OK, is a person who enjoys art in its many forms. From drawing; to reading books, writing poetry, etc. Trai believes the creative abilities in us can be let loose in many avenues and it's usually a fun experience.

One of the most thrilling things for Trai is the art of storytelling. While learning and experimenting with many different styles, Trai plans to en devour in many schemes to further develop his artistic approach.

CANDY J WEEKS

Candy J Weeks is a Tulsa native born to Lisa Weeks and Leroy Goree who are also both also from Oklahoma. A Medical Assistant since 2006 who's niche has always been Patient/Customer Service. Oddly enough she is an introvert to the core thus where her love of poetry comes in. Finding solace more in writing, you may rarely catch her on a stage. Candy's works include: this one, The Roux vol. 1 and many other unpublished works to come!

www.ingramcontent.com/pod-product-compliance
Lightning Source LLC
Chambersburg PA
CBHW071129090426
42736CB00012B/2070